AN EDUCATIONAL COLOR

99 INTERESTING
OCCUPATIONS

When I grow up
I want to be...

Tolik Trishkin

ILLUSTraTed By ToLiK TriSHKiN
DeSigNed by SaraH JaNiSSe BroWN

My Notes:

My Notes:

My Notes:

My Notes:

_____

_____

_____

_____

_____

_____

_____

_____

_____

_____

_____

_____

_____

_____

_____

_____

_____

_____

_____

_____

My Notes:

My Notes:

My Notes:

My Notes:

_____
_____
_____
_____
_____
_____
_____
_____
_____
_____
_____
_____
_____
_____
_____
_____
_____

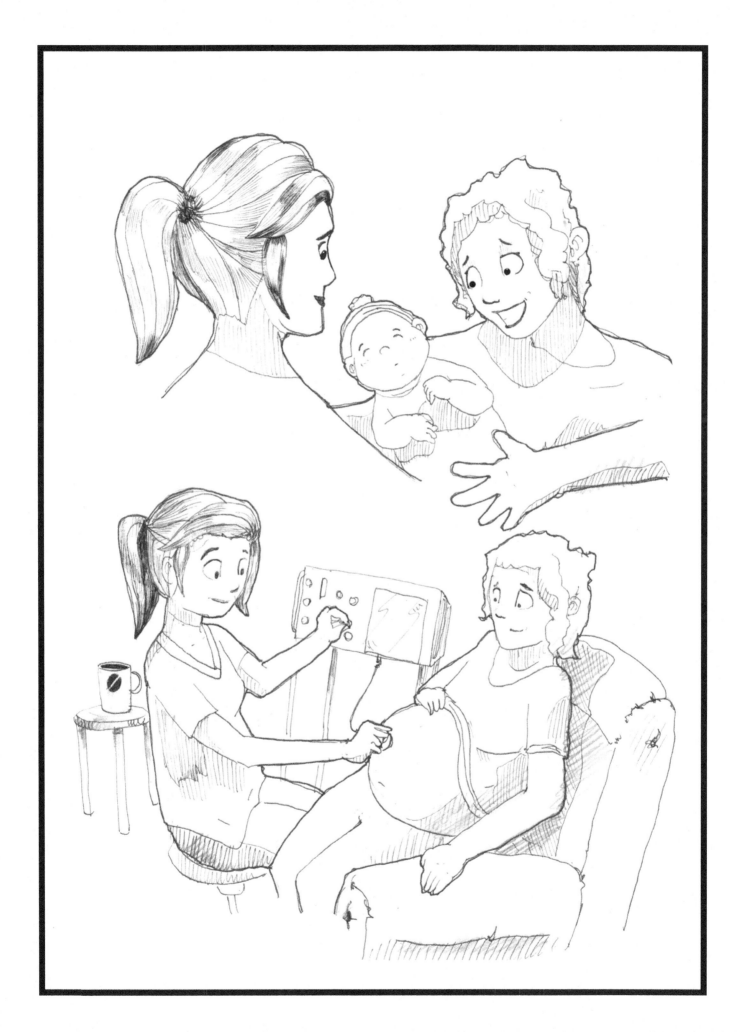

My Notes:

My Notes:

My Notes:

My Notes:

My Notes:

My Notes:

My Notes:

My Notes:

My Notes:

My Notes:

My Notes:

My Notes:

My Notes:

My Notes:

My Notes:

My Notes:

My Notes:

My Notes:

My Notes:

My Notes:

My Notes:

My Notes:

My Notes:

My Notes:

My Notes:

My Notes:

My Notes:

My Notes:

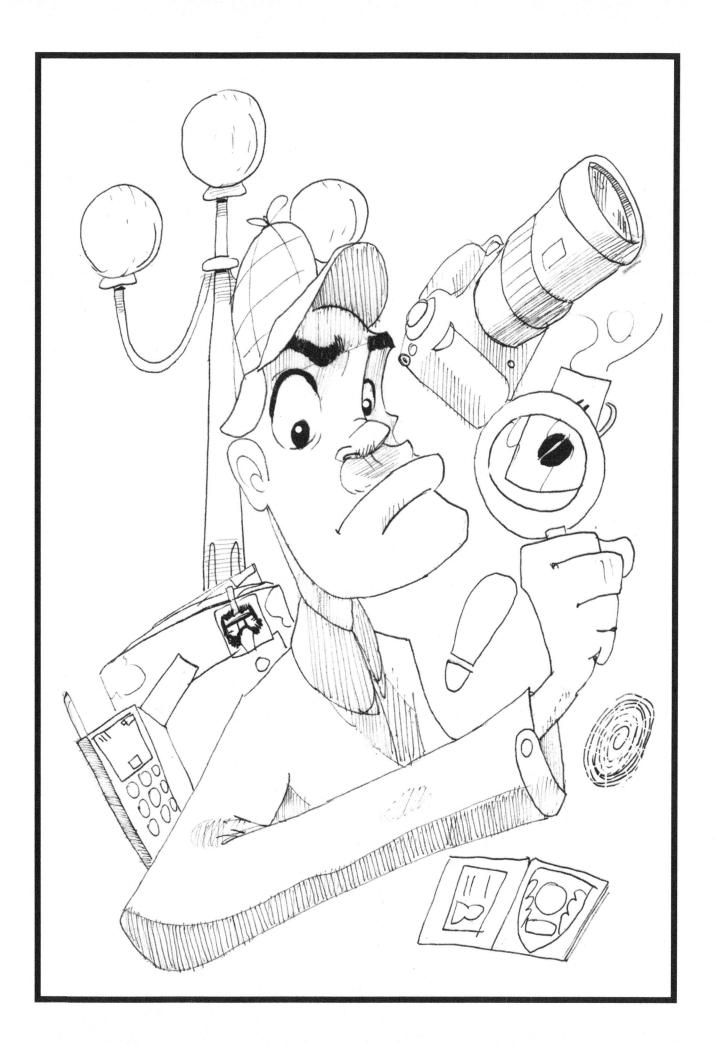

My Notes:

My Notes:

My Notes:

My Notes:

My Notes:

My Notes:

My Notes:

My Notes:

My Notes:

My Notes:

My Notes:

My Notes:

My Notes:

My Notes:

My Notes:

My Notes:

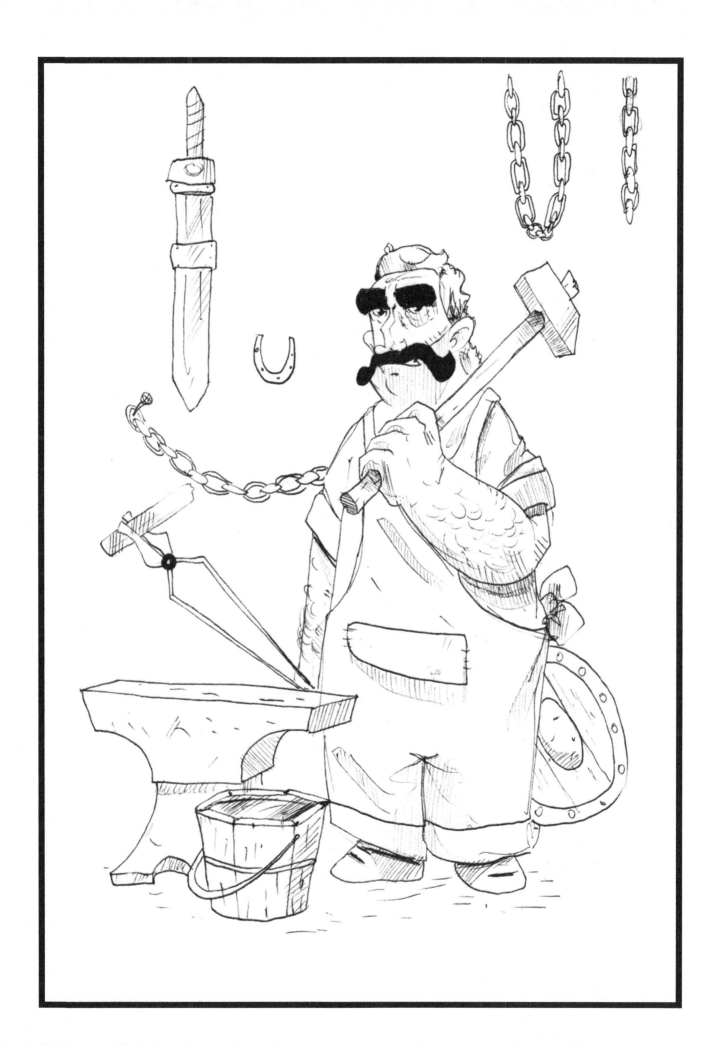

My Notes:

My Notes:

My Notes:

My Notes:

My Notes:

My Notes:

My Notes:

My Notes:

My Notes:

My Notes:

My Notes:

My Notes:

My Notes:

My Notes:

My Notes:

My Notes:

My Notes:

My Notes:

My Notes:

My Notes:

My Notes:

My Notes:

My Notes:

My Notes:

My Notes:

My Notes:

_____
_____
_____
_____
_____
_____
_____
_____
_____
_____
_____
_____
_____
_____
_____
_____
_____

My Notes:

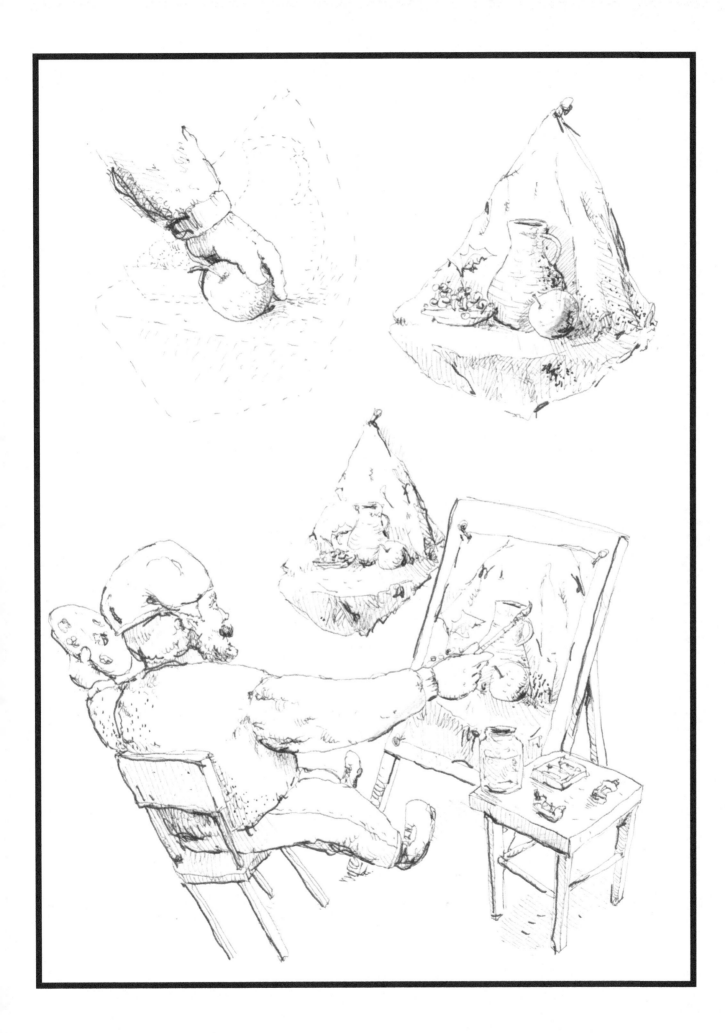

My Notes:

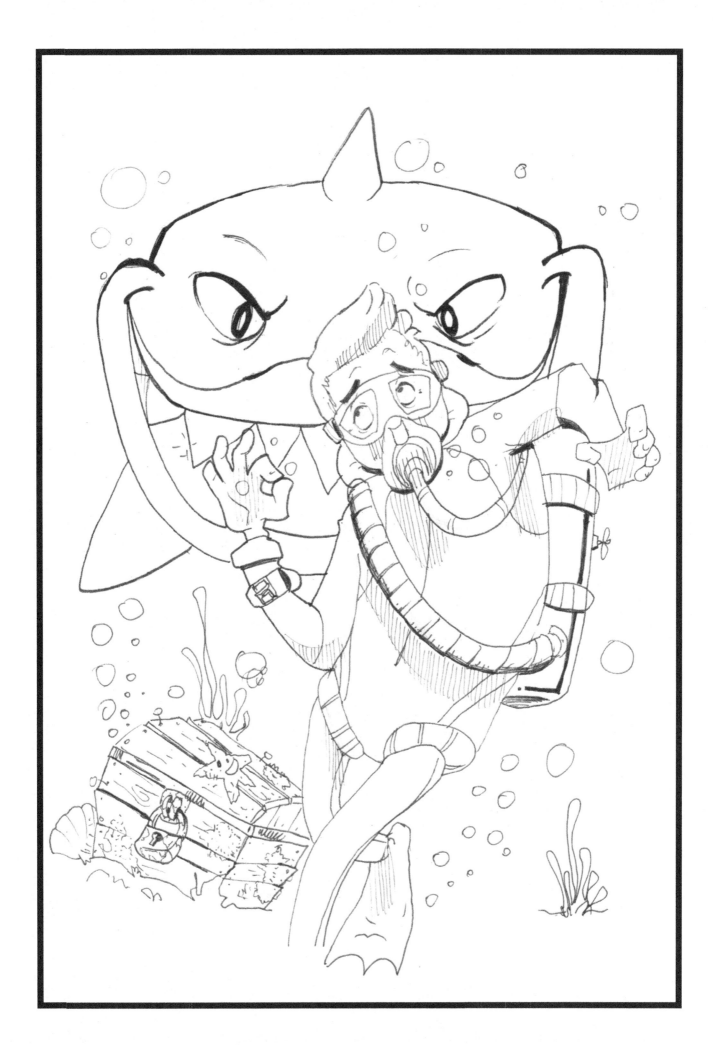

My Notes:

My Notes:

My Notes:

My Notes:

My Notes:

My Notes:

My Notes:

My Notes:

My Notes:

My Notes:

My Notes:

My Notes:

My Notes:

My Notes:

My Notes:

My Notes:

My Notes:

My Notes:

My Notes:

My Notes:

My Notes:

My Notes:

Do It Yourself
Fun-Schooling

Copyright Information

Contact Us:

The Thinking Tree LLC

617 N. Swope St. Greenfield, IN 46140. United States

317.622.8852 PHONE (Dial +1 outside of the USA) 267.712.7889 FAX

www.DyslexiaGames.com

jbrown@DyslexiaGames.com

Made in the USA
Las Vegas, NV
05 March 2024